You've Got This, Mama

IDEAS FOR TAKING CARE OF YOURSELF
WHILE YOU'RE TAKING CARE OF
YOUR LITTLE ONE

Andrea Faulkner Williams

Head Mama and Co-Founder of
Tubby Todd Bath Co.

© 2018 by Andrea Faulkner Williams

Copyright © 2018 by Tubby Todd Bath Co.
All rights reserved. This book or any portion thereof may not be reproduced or used in any manner whatsoever without the express written permission of the publisher except for the use of brief quotations in a book review.

ISBN: 978-63106-386-2

Author: Andrea Faulkner Williams
Copy Editor: Koseli Cummings
Illustrator and Designer: Erica Tighe
Editors: Mindi Bullick, Marilyn Faulkner, Heidi Saucier

TO THE TUBBY TODD MAMA COMMUNITY

May your Netflix subscription be active, your gal pals be many, and your bathtubs be hot.

Thank you for loving our products just as much as we do. This book is dedicated to you and the endless, often unrecognized, hours you spend taking care of your little ones. We see you, Mama, and we are amazed by you!

xx
Andrea

LOOK FOR THESE SYMBOLS TO JOURNAL, VISUALIZE, ANALYZE, AND CONNECT THE DOTS.

 JOURNAL PROMPT

 MAMA TIPS

 REMEMBER THIS

 VISUALIZATION ACTIVITY

 SELF-ANALYSIS QUIZ

 FAVORITE RESOURCES

 SELF-CARE TIPS

 MAMA WHO KNOWS

TABLE OF CONTENTS

1. YOU WERE MEANT FOR THIS, MAMA P. 11
2. TAKING CARE OF YOU P. 25
3. THE POSTPARTUM ROLLERCOASTER P. 39
4. WORK THAT NAUGHTY MOMMY BODY P. 57
5. TO WORK OR NOT TO WORK, AND WHAT TO DO ALL DAY P. 69
6. THERE'S NO PLACE LIKE HOME P. 85
7. KEEP THE END IN MIND P. 103
8. HOW TO BUILD A VILLAGE P. 119

THIS BOOK WAS MADE WITH LOVE

Andrea Faulkner Williams

Andrea Faulkner Williams is the head mama and co-founder of Tubby Todd Bath Co. Before launching Tubby Todd, she published her first book, *Tell Me About It, Sister! A Guide for Returned Sister Missionaries*. She is fueled by Latin pop music and a love for connecting with others. She lives in San Diego with her husband, Brian, and three little ones. Connect with Andrea on Instagram @andreafaulknerwilliams.

Koseli Cummings

Many of the activities and narratives found in this book were written by Koseli Cummings, and without her contributions this book would not have been possible. Koseli is a mother of three and lives in Berkeley, California. Everything Koseli touches becomes soft and sweet, because her goodness is unstoppable. Connect with Koseli on Instagram @koswriter.

Erica Tighe

Erica is a designer and illustrator based in Los Angeles, California. Erica's beautiful illustration style has brought the activities in this book to life. Erica believes that "beauty will save the world," and we agree that her illustrations here will save one mama at a time. Connect with Erica on Instagram @beaheartdesign.

About this Book

A few years ago, when my husband Brian and I started Tubby Todd, we saw it as a solution for our little ones' sensitive skin and a fun way to work together. But it has grown into something more powerful than we could have ever imagined. To our surprise, these all-natural skin care products have facilitated the creation of a beautiful community where mamas can connect on how to care for their little ones and themselves. I wrote this book because I love the Tubby Todd Mamas!

From this online community we've seen the need for a more supportive, non-judgemental place for women to share their concerns. As Mamas we know that we will not ever be able to fully care for our little ones until we are first caring for ourselves, but sometimes it is difficult to make self-care a priority. So in order to support our Tubby Todd Mama community, we've collected the best advice from experts into a personal guide that will shed new light on the mysterious world of self-care as a mother. This guide provides exercises, tools, and personal anecdotes to help busy moms find the mental, emotional, and physical strength they need. Our goal is to leave our Mamas energized and more capable of caring for their families and themselves.

You Mamas are sincere and committed to providing the best care for your little ones. I love and honor that in each of you. Between work, social media, housework, spit up, caring for your partner, and health challenges, life can be ROUGH. We need a little reminder that we got this—and, we're actually doing a freaking good job! Because we are, right? Right!

All the love, Mama,

xx
Andrea

Andrea Faulkner Williams
December 2017

For my babies: Jo, Walker T. & Jamie

I LOVE YOU THIIIIIS MUCH.

ONE.

You were meant for this, Mama

intention:

THE GOAL OF THIS CHAPTER IS TO HELP YOU REMEMBER THAT YOU WERE MEANT FOR THIS ROLE AS A MOTHER, AND YOUR LITTLE ONE IS LUCKY TO CALL YOU MAMA.

> I REALIZED THAT IN EVERY STEP AS A MOM, NO MATTER HOW MANY KIDS YOU HAVE, AND NO MATTER WHAT STAGE OF LIFE YOU'RE IN, MOST THINGS WILL FEEL NEW AND EVEN A LITTLE BIT SCARY.

A week after James was born, I sent my mom, who was staying with me, away for the afternoon because I was positive I had everything under control. Soon after she left, I decided that James needed his first bath, and the first thought that came to my mind was: "Wait, how do I bathe a newborn? I need my mom to come back!" Ha! This was a little surprising because James is my third baby, and oh, don't forget…I OWN a bath company. But still, I somehow felt intimidated and overwhelmed at the challenge of bathing this new, precious package all by myself.

It was a humbling moment and I realized that in every step as a mom, no matter how many kids you have, and no matter what stage of life you're in, most things will feel new and even a little bit scary. You love these little ones so much and sometimes that love pushes you to a fear that you might be doing something wrong. So, if you're feeling overwhelmed or uncertain about your role as a mother, I hope you remember that you were meant for this.

Whenever I'm feeling inadequate as a mom, it is helpful for me to stop and focus on what I am actually working toward. Feelings of inadequacy have little to do with our capabilities and are usually directly correlated to an expectation we have imposed on ourselves.

Let's ask, "Have I set an unobtainable standard for myself and my little ones? If so, then let's replace that standard with a realistic goal of day-to-day work and progress that will lead to success for everyone.

You already have everything your children need within you.

I hope the thoughts and exercises found in this chapter will rekindle your belief that you already have everything your children need within you. Replace any unrealistic expectations with kind insights about your talents and what makes you, you. Refer back to them on tough mom days.

Here's to more focused time spent with our kids and fewer regrets thinking about the type of mom we should be or wish we were. Here's to accepting our situation—whatever stage of life we're in—and working to make it the very best for ourselves and for our families. Here's to realizing that at the end of the day all that matters is that our kids know how much we truly love them. You, Mama, are an incredible mom. You were meant for this, and your little ones are lucky to call you theirs.

xx
Andrea

A mother's love for her child is like nothing else in the world.

IT KNOWS NO LAW, NO PITY, IT DATES ALL THINGS AND CRUSHES DOWN REMORSELESSLY ALL THAT STANDS IN ITS PATH.

AGATHA CHRISTIE

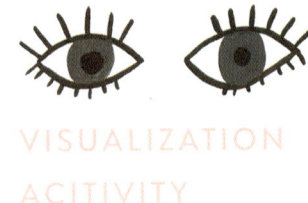

VISUALIZATION
ACITIVITY

THEIR NEEDS

Stop. Think about what your child(ren) actually need at this moment. Not just the physical necessities, but what do they need from you as their mom in this moment? Complete the next steps for each of your children individually.

YOUR CHILD'S NEED

_____
_____
_____
_____
_____
_____
_____
_____
_____
_____
_____
_____

STEP 1   Draw your child(ren)
STEP 2   List their needs
STEP 3   Connect their needs to what you can do as their mom. Draw a line from either your head, heart, lips, ears, or hands to your child's specific need.

YOUR CHILD'S NEEDS

_____
_____
_____
_____
_____
_____
_____
_____
_____
_____
_____
_____
_____
_____

YOUR CHILD'S NEEDS

_____

_____

_____

_____

_____

_____

_____

_____

_____

_____

_____

_____

_____

_____

YOUR CHILD'S NEEDS

_____
_____
_____
_____
_____
_____
_____
_____
_____
_____
_____
_____
_____
_____

25 BILLION MOTHERS IN THE WORLD

25 MILLION MOTHERS IN THE UNITED STATES

130 MILLION BABIES ARE BORN EVERY YEAR

4.3 BABIES ARE BORN EVERY SECOND

You are NOT alone.

MAMA tips

WHAT DO YOU LOVE?

Do something you love today. Whether it's reading a good book, calling your BFF to catch up, or getting a pedicure, do something fun that makes you happy.

FAVORITE RESOURCES

BABIES DOCUMENTARY
Sweetest look at motherhood around the world. A good reminder that we are not alone.

TUBBY TODD MAMAS FACEBOOK GROUP
Looking for an uplifting group of mom friends? Search "Tubby Todd Mamas" on Facebook and request to join. Ask anything under the sun.

MAMA WHO KNOWS

What's your best advice for a new mom who is feeling uncertain in her role as a mom?

Although everyone (including the old man in line at the grocery store who never had kids) will have ample advice for you, only listen to the people you truly trust and, most importantly, give yourself space to listen to your own intuition. Not having a lot of experience as a caregiver before becoming a mother, I remember the idea of a "mother's intuition" being somewhat laughable to me as I sat in the hospital with my firstborn, with absolutely no idea what to do next. Over the years, however, I have realized that, for me, "motherly intuition" has usually just meant turning down the volume on anxiety and worry so I can tune in to my baby's needs. When I create that space, some kind of an answer comes. Despite what marketing and social media may tell you, there is no one way to be a great mom. Being the best YOU is the best and most authentic gift you can give your children.

is the founder and CEO of Solly Baby and co-founder of ARQ. A mother of four, she and her family live in San Diego, CA. Everything Elle does looks beautiful and effortless, especially being a mom, and that takes a lot of work! But our favorite thing about Elle is how seriously she takes her responsibility as a mother to her four little ones Lucy, Solomon, Frances & Hazel. Connect with Elle on Instagram @ellerowley

ZOOM OUT Sometimes it's hard to see what's actually true when we're too close. Take a step back. Imagine you're looking at yourself through the eyes of your little one(s). How do they see you? Write free form all the things they see when they look at your face, hands, and heart. Sit with your feelings and let yourself feel the love of your little one(s) and how they see you.

EVERYTHING YOUR CHILD NEEDS LIVES WITHIN YOU.

TWO.

Taking Care of You

THE GOAL OF THIS CHAPTER IS TO HELP YOU MAKE SELF-CARE A DAILY PRIORITY.

THE BEST GIFT YOU CAN GIVE YOUR FAMILY IS YOUR OWN HAPPINESS.

When I was 26 weeks pregnant with my third baby my nausea returned (Hooray!), and I began experiencing extreme headaches. The sickness began to take a toll on me emotionally and I felt like I was riding a hormonal roller coaster all day long, every single day. Instead of thinking "Hey, Andrea you're 26 weeks pregnant with your third child and have a lot of people who rely on you. What can we do to get you feeling better?" I started obsessing over everything I had been neglecting. I worried about practicing letters more with my five year old, coloring with my two year old, and how many unanswered emails brimmed in my inbox. Sounds like productive thoughts for a depressed preggo, right? One night while lying in bed I read an article that made me realize something—no matter how many emails I answered, or how many letters I taught my children, none of that would mean anything if I wasn't taking care of myself first. I reached out for help, started to prioritize my own health, and within weeks felt dramatically better. It turns out that I needed new acid reflux medicine more than I needed to question my worth!

No matter how many kids you have, how old they are, whether you're struggling with infertility or considering surrogacy or adoption; whether you've got a career or you're a SAHM or somewhere in between; no matter where you live and with however many people, it's crucial you take care of yourself. I hope this chapter helps you consider the most pressing needs in your life right now. Sometimes the most challenging part of taking care of yourself is knowing what you need to do to start. So, take a deep breath. (Did you really take a deep breath? No? Do it with me right now…feels good, right?!) In these next few pages I hope you find your next steps to better self-care. Do you need to join the gym? Watch something funny? Start writing that book you've always dreamt of writing? Make something with your hands? Eat a gorgeous salad? Get a babysitter for an afternoon? Or take steps to start the business idea you have? Or best of all…TAKE A NAP?! Over and over again I learn that the best thing I can do for my kids is take better care of myself, so I can take better care of them. At first these two concepts seem contradictory, but they actually go hand in hand. We must recognize that we are best suited to care for others when we are able to treat ourselves gently, nurture our bodies, and feed our brains and spirits. It's up to us to take care of ourselves—because you and I both know, nobody else is going to do it for us! #amen

xx
Andrea

VISUALIZATION ACITIVITY

Draw a HAPPY mom. What does she look like?
What is she wearing? What has she eaten? Is she sleeping?
How does she spend her free time?

You are NOT alone.

THE CHALLENGE OF PRIORITIZING SELF-CARE

Resolving Assertiveness Concerns, Dr. Julie de Azevedo Hanks, LCSW

In my years as a therapist, I've found that the biggest obstacle for women concerning assertiveness is the fear that it will hurt their relationships. Many are scared that speaking up and expressing difference will cause harm or disruption in how they connect with others. That is always a risk we take, but the people in our lives that are worth being close to won't abandon us in the face of conflict or disagreement. Yes, it can be uncomfortable, and there's likely emotional work that needs to be done, but assertiveness is the key to showing up, being heard, and presenting your most authentic self, which will ultimately result in healthier and stronger relationships."

Dynamic self-help & relationship expert Dr. Julie de Azevedo Hanks, LCSW, loves to make a difference for women. Her advice has been featured nationally, including in *The Wall Street Journal*, *Parenting* magazine, Fox News, and others.

SELF-ANALYSIS QUIZ

Honestly analyze how you're doing in each area, then make a quick plan for change if needed.

How am I doing?

	NEVER ONCE	HARDLY EVER	SOME DAYS	TOTALLY!
Wore something other than black yoga pants	O	O	O	O
Worked hard, played hard	O	O	O	O
Did something you wanted to do just for you	O	O	O	O
Ate a well-balanced meal while sitting down (while it was still hot)	O	O	O	O
Made the doctor's appointment(s) you need to make	O	O	O	O
Locked yourself in the bathroom to relax	O	O	O	O
Laughed (really hard)	O	O	O	O
Took a break from social media and read a book	O	O	O	O
Said No when you weren't feeling it	O	O	O	O
Sat in silence	O	O	O	O

SELF-ANALYSIS QUIZ

These are the things that make me feel like I'm not holding up (but mean nothing):

How am I doing?

	TOTALLY!	SOME DAYS	HARDLY EVER	NEVER ONCE
Made random lists of to-dos that have no real consequence (organize pictures on your laptop, color-sort your toddler's toys, post on Facebook)	O	O	O	O
Checked social media accounts that are critical, overbearing, or not in line with my beliefs	O	O	O	O
Spent time with people who have pessimistic, victimized attitudes	O	O	O	O
Engaged in black-and-white patterns of thinking (e.g. "I always drop the ball." "I never keep up with my exercise routine.")	O	O	O	O

How much is too much? Think of a day when you felt like you ran around like a chicken with its head cut off. Let's rewind and think through that day and find the places where you should have said NO. What are your trigger points? Write them down. For example: "I know I've taken it too far when I haven't slept enough, eaten a good meal all day, finished my work for the day, etc."

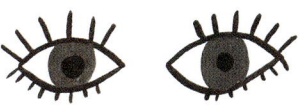

VISUALIZATION ACITIVITY

WHAT CAN YOU SKIP IN ORDER TO GIVE YOURSELF SOME BREATHING ROOM?

Write down what you don't need by the trash can. (Soccer practice, piano lessons, reality TV, 24/7 availability to anyone who texts you, checking Instagram whenever you're bored, community responsibilities, diets, a spotless house, etc.) Check-in with yourself whenever unsettled feelings surface.

MAMA WHO KNOWS

How did you learn to make taking care of yourself a priority as a mom?

"Real talk? I've smacked my head against a wall, ON PURPOSE, because my brain felt so crazy and out of control. At the same time, I just wanted the racing thoughts and anxiety to stop, and smacking my forehead felt like it might help. It didn't. It gave me a headache. And what did I do after that? Call for help? Text my husband that I had reached a limit, or cut out some commitments? Nope. I reapplied the mascara I had cried off and committed to throwing another 700-person dance party. Luckily, I am no longer this woman. And you don't have to be her either. At the time, I just wanted to please everyone and get a lot accomplished! I just wanted everyone to be happy. Even if I was making dents in my wall with my head.

But I have a question for you. When you are in a depressed, anxious or frantic state…who are you capable of thinking about? YOU! It's all about YOU. So why is it that even the phrase "self-care" can make us feel guilty and selfish? I'll tell you why. Because somewhere down the line, we decided that being women, caretakers, and nurturers *meant we could only take care of OTHER people. Really what it means is we should be the VERY best at taking care of ourselves. Neglecting self-care usually results in those anxious, depressed, frantic, and overwhelmed states—the kind that lead to forehead smacking or sometimes something worse.*

I hope with all my heart you're not in as extreme a position as I was in. But do you know how I got there? By ignoring self-care in small ways for a long time and not realizing incorrect thought patterns. Start today. Call for help if you need it, break a commitment, read a book, or take a nap. The world needs you at your best, and you really do deserve not to be miserable. Oh, and only you can be you -- and you're already as awesome as you need to be. You can do this.

ALISON Faulkner is a podcaster, speaker, brand strategist & motivator. You probably know her from her online branding courses or her inappropriate Instagram dancing, but we know her as a powerful force for helping others achieve their dreams—all while dancing in a bedazzled sports bra. Alison lives in Provo, UT with her husband Eric and her three children, Ginger, Rad and Fiona. Connect with Alison on Instagram @thealisonshow.

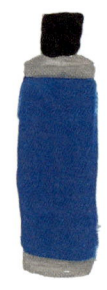

SELF-CARE TIPS

3 STEPS TO YOU TIME

What are 3 things you can do in the next 24 hours to give yourself what you need?

For example: hire a babysitter for 3 hours, go to bed by 8 PM, hire a cleaning crew once a month, create a meal plan, enroll your toddler in preschool. Maybe it's something more fun: write a letter, read a good book, splurge on Egyption cotton 800-thread-count sheets, or order your favorite ice cream on Amazon Prime Now. Maybe it's just this: do something that makes you gloriously happy in a deep, I-am-giggling-all-by-myself kind of way.

1. _____

2. _____

3. _____

NOW PUT THEM ON YOUR TO DO LIST.

MAMA *tips*

PLEASURE IS GOOD, PLEASURE IS HAPPY

What do you like to do? Set a goal to do something fun every day. Have a dance competition with your kids, plan a black-tie dinner party, send a thoughtful email, sit in the dark, organize a drawer. Whatever gives you that buzzy, "I am living!" feeling, do it and do it often. Sometimes we think of being with kids as work, and time alone or with friends as fun. Can you find more ways to add fun to your time with your little ones?

BE GENTLE WITH YOURSELF. MAKE TIME EVERYDAY TO CARE FOR YOURSELF AND DO THINGS YOU LOVE.

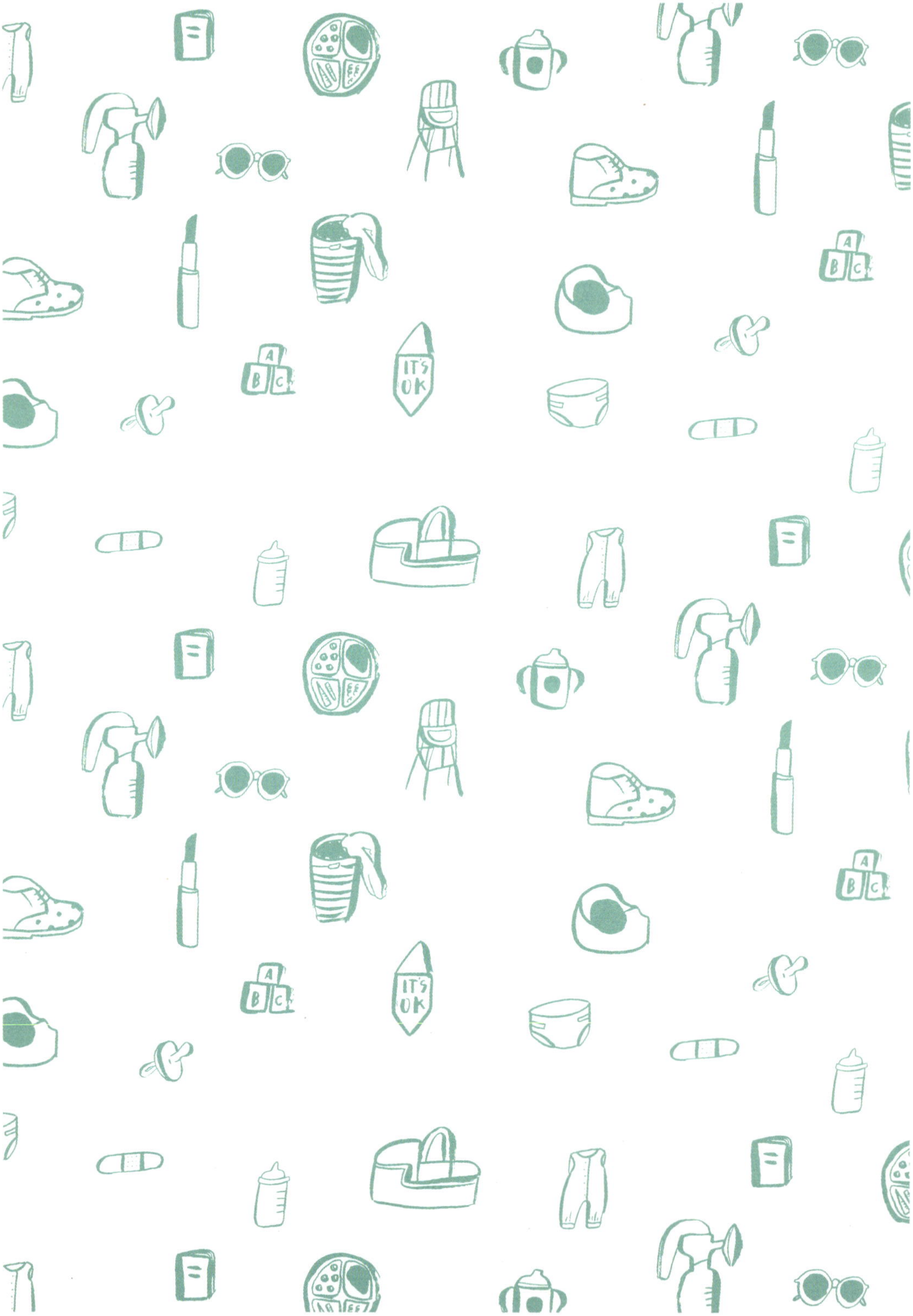
IT'S OK
IT'S OK

THREE.

THE POSTPARTUM ROLLER COASTER

intention:

THE GOAL OF THIS CHAPTER IS TO HELP YOU ASSESS WHERE YOU ARE EMOTIONALLY AND PHYSICALLY IN YOUR POSTPARTUM RECOVERY.

IF I WANT TO ENJOY AND CARE FOR MY LITTLE ONES IN THAT PRECIOUS TIME, I NEED TO CARE FOR MYSELF.

The week I had my first baby, my sister-in-law sent me an email that changed my postpartum recovery. She said that I should give myself a fourth trimester—that I should allow myself a minimum of three months before I started to wonder if my jeans fit, expected myself to get back to any resemblance of a schedule, or pushed any goals on myself. This sweet invitation meant so much to me as a brand new mom, and I clung to those words and forced thoughts of "recovery" and "bouncing back" out of my mind whenever I began feeling discouraged in my first few months postpartum.

Six years and three postpartum recoveries later, I clearly see the flaws in our Western culture's approach to new mothers. We applaud women who are out with their newborns and expect new moms to "bounce back" within weeks, return to household duties, and resume their jobs.

After recognizing this backward perspective, I made a conscious effort to stay home longer and do less after the birth of my third child. As a result, I had the happiest and strongest transition back into my daily routine with that birth. Although in my previous births I had tried to be free of expectations, I did not realize that I physically had taken on too much: too many outings and planned social activities; not enough time at home. With my third birth, instead of feeling that we needed to get out of the house, I made excuses about why we needed to stay in.

When people would ask me how it was possible to stay indoors—in my bed—for almost four entire weeks when we had three small children, my answer was, **because I decided to**.

"I decided to."

In those weeks I read a lot of books and watched a lot of movies in bed with my two older children. I asked friends and my church group to help arrange playdates and meals. My extended family helped. My husband (who returned to work just a few days after the baby was born) took over housework and carpools on days he was home. I worked with my team at work to plan ahead so I could take some time off. It was tough in a small business, but it was possible.

We all know that babies don't keep; the newborn days are gone before you know it. But something I have also come to honor and respect is the health of my body and soul. Our bodies are not indestructible. If I want to enjoy and care for my little ones in that precious time, I need to care for myself. I hope that during this chapter you are able to find the resources you need to help you take care of you and your little one during the fourth trimester. And wherever you are in your postpartum recovery, I encourage you to honestly assess your physical and emotional needs and take active steps to care for yourself. I think you will be happy to find that in many cases, caring for yourself means getting back in bed, foregoing all responsibility, and holding that little baby close. Now that, Mama, is the best job in the world, right?

xx
Andrea

The wound is the place the LIGHT enters you.

RUMI

Postpartum Healing Tips

MAMA tips

1. Get a "nursty" (aka humongous water bottle w/ tons of ice and a straw)

2. Use Tubby Todd All Over Ointment on your c-section scar and cover with pads (change pads multiple times a day)

3. Make padsicles: Freeze thick pads + Tucks. Change your padsicle EVERY time you go to the bathroom. This keeps the inflammation down and soothes any healing stitches, tears, etc.

4. Take lots of Sitz baths. (Basically just warm shallow baths for your lady parts.)

5. Get skin-to-skin with your newborn: It helps you heal, bonds you to baby, and is super yummy. Let yourself just die a little over that newborn smell. (Crying a little here just thinking about it.)

6. Take a break NOW: Sit on the porch, lay on a blanket in your backyard, take a walk around the neighborhood (or to your mailbox), call your mom and cry while driving to get a gallon of ice cream. But promise me you'll leave that baby with someone you trust for 5-20 minutes as soon as you're ready to get a little breather. Newborn crying, poop, new-mom anxiety, birth recovery, and utter exhaustion are beasts, and you've got to be proactive to keep your head on straight. Don't try to be a hero.

> If you've had a baby and you're in pain: GET HELP. Ask questions. Pester your doctor. Find answers until you get the physical therapy, internal pelvic floor therapy, back massage, hip realignment, medicine, talk therapy, and/or specialized resources you need to feel like yourself again. You're worth it. Make YOU your top priority. Channel your inner Mama Bear to fight for what you need.

FAVORITE RESOURCES

First Forty Days: The Essential Art of Nurturing the New Mother by Heng Ou. A fascinating exploration of how we can take better care of mothers after birth.

The Mama Blog www.tubbytodd.com/blogs/tubby-blog

Postpartum Support International
(www.postpartum.net) Essential info about perinatal mood & anxiety disorders, including risk factors, symptoms & treatments.

Heal Pelvic Pain by Amy Stein

The Longest Shortest Time Podcast
Episodes: Healing after Childbirth and Risky Birth-ness
www.longestshortesttime.com/episode-110-risky-birth-ness/
www.longestshortesttime.com/podcast-49-healing-after-childbirth/

Ask your closest gal pals about their favorite ways to heal postpartum and list them here.

MAMAS WHO KNOW:
4 MOMS ON POSTPARTUM HEALING

PELVIC FLOOR THERAPY
Rachel, Age 24

After the birth of my second baby, I was diagnosed by a urogynecologist with grade 2 rectocele prolapse (pelvic floor no longer supports the rectum), over-active bladder, and pelvic floor dysfunction. She also discovered internal scar tissue and perineal scar tissue where I tore from my first birth. I started pelvic floor physical therapy, where I learned just how important the pelvic floor is and how it can be affected by the way we hold our body. I was able to become asymptomatic with my prolapse, close my Diastasis recti from 3 finger widths to 1.5, and learn proper body mechanics to keep my pelvic floor happy. My physical therapist was an angel to me. She truly improved the quality of my life and my marriage.

BIRTH CONTROL DRAMA
Koseli, Age 29

After getting an IUD (intrauterine device) six weeks postpartum, I experienced a pinched feeling in my left lower abdomen. It would come and go but it just felt a little off to me. I had my IUD checked and they said it was fine. The pinching sensation continued for weeks until I went back and insisted something felt off. They did an ultra-sound and found the IUD had embedded in my uterine lining and needed to be removed immediately. It was a low-risk, non-invasive surgery, but I still felt grateful and relieved that I trusted my lady gut to literally tell me that something wasn't right.

ORGAN PROLAPSE
Lauren, Age 27

I had a textbook pregnancy until 38 weeks when I developed preeclampsia. Delivery was rough, and I ended up with pelvic organ prolapse. I had never even heard of it. I discovered it on my own (which was terrifying, and Dr. Google didn't help) and mentioned it to my OBGYN at my 6-week appointment. He said, "It's not that bad. Do some kegels and you're fine to go for a run. You can always have surgery." Absolutely horrible advice. Surgery options are lacking and not often successful. I found a support group on FB and have a PT consultation next month. It's altered how I live. I no longer run. I can't use tampons. I feel pain and heaviness when I carry my daughter or do any heavy lifting. Despite this, I am hopeful that with PT things will improve."

ROUGH EPISIOTOMY HEALING
Kerstin, Age 26

Nineteen months ago I had an emergency episiotomy. I needed a vacuum assisted delivery because my son quite literally got stuck, and I ended up with a third-degree tear.

Recovery from the episiotomy and tearing was much more difficult than I anticipated. While my incision healed quickly, it took weeks for the muscles to heal and the pain to completely go away. I was initially discouraged that friends who had babies at the same time as me were back to exercising and normal activities by 6 weeks postpartum. It took me closer to 10 weeks postpartum to even feel like I wanted to resume those activities. It really helped me to remember that I tore a muscle in a very sensitive area of my body, and to be gentle on myself (physically and emotionally).

MAMA WHO KNOWS

How can women prioritize postpartum healing?

Prioritizing postpartum healing really begins with seeing your body beyond the extra weight and embracing the fourth trimester. The first three months are nature's built-in time to heal, and the power to heal is yours. Those things that seem so simple like rest, breathing, and gentle, specific movement are so valuable on a number of levels during this time. Do everything in your power to avoid comparing your healing to another woman's and do what you need to do to care for your body & mind.

JENNY Redford

is a Pilates-teaching mama and creator of Hello Body Pilates. She educates women on clear, simple postpartum recovery. She lives with her husband and two little ones, Penn and Thea, in San Diego, CA. Connect with Jenny on Instagram @hellobodypilates.

You are N⊙T alone.

1 IN 7
PREGNANT AND NEW MOMS WILL HAVE A PERINATAL MOOD OR ANXIETY DISORDER

1 IN 4
AMERICAN WOMEN SUFFERS FROM A PELVIC FLOOR ISSUE AT SOME POINT IN HER LIFE

3.3 MILLION
WOMEN IN THE U.S. EXPERIENCE PELVIC ORGAN PROLAPSE**

40-70%
OF WOMEN HAVE URINARY INCONTINENCE**

PELVIC FLOOR THERAPY HAS ONLY BEEN AROUND SINCE THE LATE 90S

81%
OF MOMS REPORT BREASTFEEDING DURING THE FIRST YEAR

49%	27%
OF THOSE BABIES ARE STILL BREASTFEEDING AT 6 MONTHS	OF THOSE BABIES ARE STILL BREASTFEEDING AT 12 MONTHS***

http://www.pelvicorganprolapsesupport.org/pelvic-organ-prolapse-help-and-hope/**
https://www.cdc.gov/breastfeeding/pdf/2014breastfeedingreportcard.pdf***

VISUALIZATION ACITIVTY

MY NOT TO-DO LIST

Go through My Not-To-Do list and replace with a practical plan of attack.

Example: ~~iron clothes~~ buy wrinkle free spray

cook dinner

have visitors

respond to comments on social media

do dishes

let other people hold your baby

go to church

RSVP to birthday party invites

wear jeans

participate in carpool

greet visitors at the door

do laundry

attend your other kids' extracurricular activities like soccer, piano, dance, etc.

check your email

clean toilets

Set boundaries before baby is born. Get clear with yourself and then communicate with crystal clarity to your partner and any others who will be on the frontline with you after Baby is born. Tell them what your expectations are for your postpartum recovery. If at all possible, enlist every person who loves you to care for the baby and especially you in some specific way.

You are NOT alone.

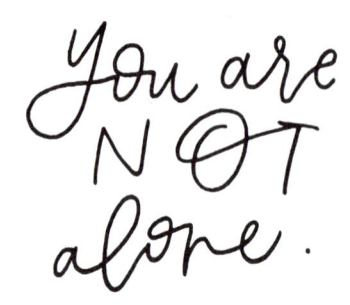

OVER HALF OF NEW MOTHERS STRUGGLE TO COPE

57%
FEEL ISOLATED

2 IN 5
MOTHERS ADMIT TO GETTING ANGRY*

900,000
WOMEN GET POST-PARTUM DEPRESSION EACH YEAR**

IN HIGH-POVERTY AREAS THE RATE OF POST-PARTUM DEPRESSION IS AS HIGH AS 25%

NSPCC*
http://postpartumprogress.org **

The First 40 Days

The Essential Art of Nourishing
the New Mother

by Heng Ou

The idea behind *The First Forty Days* is that
we should be giving mothers a softer place to
land after having a baby. Besides the physical
task of pregnancy, birth, and recovery, there is
an emotional element to recovery that is rarely
addressed. This book is full of practical advice
on how to create necessary space for healing
after birth, as well as recipes to encourage
recuperation and calm. It's a beautiful and
refreshing guide for a new mom navigating the
postpartum period.

journal prompt

One of the best things for a mom's mental health is getting all those free-floating anxieties, thoughts, worries, and plans out of your head and onto paper. Here are a couple prompts to get you started:

How did your birth(s) make you feel? Do you feel like you're still processing it?

What are you most surprised about that's happening in your life right now? What do you feel like you need help with?

How are you doing? No, how are you really doing?
List all your worries. Go ahead. Brain dump.

MOTHERHOOD IS FULL OF
EVER-CHANGING SEASONS.
FIND PEOPLE TO PUT ON YOUR "TEAM" TO
HELP YOU AND YOUR FAMILY. STRONG WOMEN
KNOW WHEN TO ASK FOR HELP.

56

FOUR.

Work that naughty mommy body

intention:

THE GOAL OF THIS CHAPTER IS TO HELP YOU MAKE TAKING CARE OF YOURSELF PHYSICALLY AN ONGOING PRIORITY.

You are beautiful, Mama.

Whether you deliver your baby vaginally or through C-section, have a surrogate or adopt—being a mom is a physical job. It requires bending, snapping, sweating and sometimes twerking. (Not sure why, but I feel like twerking is inevitable, right?) You will be peed on, spit up on, and even pooped on. With very little sleep (and even less time to take a shower) the physical demands of being a mama to little ones can get real. My body is no longer the same as it was before I brought my first little one into the world seven years ago. It obviously has changed physically, but more than anything it has more purpose and need to function properly than ever before in my life. My health and my daily physical routine affect the life of every single person around me. And that makes me feel so strong! It makes me feel sexy and beautiful for the right reasons. Taking care of my body has become a passion for me because missing my dentist appointments or workouts changes the way I can care for others—and caring for others gives me purpose in a way I had never dreamed of.

Don't get me wrong—there have been moments of horror when I have had to accept my saggy boobs, stretch marks, and hips that are a few inches wider than they used to be. Sound familiar? And then there's the pee! Not just my kids peeing on me (which has happened more times than I care to count) but me—peeing my pants all of the time. I am reminded daily of my postpartum body each time I cough, sneeze, laugh or jump. And although I laugh, when I talk about these (more serious) postpartum issues, I want you to know I take them seriously. I have cried, seen doctors, and spent many hours talking to my husband and girlfriends about what my body has been through. Sometimes it feels easier to ignore postpartum complications instead of taking care of them, but life is better when I try my best to put my big girl panties on (and possibly maybe a diaper too?) and face them head on.

You are beautiful, Mama, and I hope in this chapter you are able to find a way to make caring for yourself a priority. Because that naughty mommy body of yours deserves all of the love you have to give it, so it can turn around and give it right back to those little ones who need you.

xx
Andrea

Being a mom has made me so tired. And so happy.

TINA FEY

MAMA WHO KNOWS

How do you make time to care for your physical body?

"I'll be honest, making time to take care of myself physically is sometimes a struggle. My work days vary and my toddler often throws me curve balls. Some days we end up eating donuts on the kitchen floor to keep us both from having a meltdown. For me, working out is a way to get out my aggressions and sweat out negativity. Getting physical leaves me with space for creativity and energy to keep up with my kids. Finding time to get a workout in looks different every week, as some days I can make it to the gym and other days I count walking to Target as a full body workout. I think the key is to do what you can, when you can, and give yourself props for it all. Mom life is hard no matter how you slice it. Making my physical health a priority has made me a better mom, sure, but it also makes me a better person overall, and I'm addicted to the feeling it gives me.

That said, I also love the way a donut tastes. So really, it's about balance and not beating yourself up if you put on yoga pants with zero intention of working out."

JACQUI Saldana

is a lifestyle and recipe blogger at babyboybakery.com She is also the creator of Baby Boy Bakery Kids. Jacqui lives in LA with her husband, Dan, and daughter, Mila, and dedicates her online space in memory of her son, Ryan Cruz. She inspires people to live a loud and wild life -- no matter what they are faced with. Connect with Jacqui on Instagram @babyboybakery.

journal prompt

What foods make you feel unstoppable?

What ways can you nurture yourself when you're having your period?

How much sleep do you need?

What makes you feel beautiful?

What helps you have positive sexual experiences?

What's your favorite way to prioritize exercise?

What outfit works every single time you wear it?

The first step in loving our bodies is knowing our bodies.

HOW TO DRESS BEFORE & AFTER BABY

Everyone talks about maternity clothes, but guys, what about after you have the baby?! You've got to have a post-birth dressing strategy. We love the capsule wardrobe idea but we have to laugh. Moms were the OG capsule wardrobe. When nothing else fits, you're left with only a couple of dresses and black yoga pants. But feeling confident and comfortable in what you're wearing goes a long way, so here are a few tips for postpartum dressing:

TEN POSTPARTUM CLOTHING ITEMS WE LOVE

Checklist

- [ ] 2 flattering t-shirts. Go for two sizes above your normal, pre-pregnancy size.
- [ ] 1 button up
- [ ] 1 caftan dress that buttons in front
- [ ] 1 knit open cardigan that falls past your bum bum
- [ ] 1 really good button-down shirt like a flattering ¾ length flannel
- [ ] Jeans that fit (Need to have at least one pair that works at any time)
- [ ] 2 pair of yoga pants
- [ ] Matching top and bottom pair of pajamas (like, real adult jammies)
- [ ] 1 top that makes you feel absolutely beautiful (good color, don't have to iron it, and you feel like a babe every single time you wear it)

What new items do you need to add to your wardrobe to help you feel beautiful and prepared each day?

_____

_____

_____

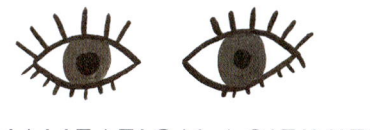

VISUALIZATION ACITIVITY

SAY THESE MANTRAS OUT LOUD.

(No, really. Try it.)

SINCE BECOMING A MOTHER, MY BODY HAS CHANGED.

MY BODY CAN NOW DO THESE THINGS:
_____

MY BODY HAS SURPRISED ME BY:
_____

I LOVE _____
ABOUT MY POSTTPARTUM BODY.

Breathe

MAMA tips

GETTING SEXY BACK

meow

Remove all phones, laptops, ipads, etc. from bedroom.

Turn off phone (yes completely off) and meet in bed at 9.

Play a strategic board game.

Talk about non-baby stuff.

Talk more about dreams, vacations, and lofty plans, and less about logistics and to-dos.

Look at old pictures together.

Laugh together.

IDEAS FOR GETTING SEXY BACK

SCENARIO 1: Every night for a week, turn your phone off, get a plate of nachos, and watch a show together in bed.

SCENARIO 2: What's something you used to love doing with your partner before you had kids that you haven't done in awhile. Do that. (i.e.: go to a concert, play tennis, watch an entire movie without falling asleep....)

SCENARIO 3: Do something thoughtful every day for a week. Write a note, bring your partner breakfast in bed, book one night in a hotel, surprise him with his favorite candy bar.

SCENARIO 4: Slip on the old wedding lingerie and wait for your partner in bed.

SCENARIO 5: Do something that makes you feel sexy, like go for a run, put on lipstick, brush your teeth, or wear high heels. Don't be afraid to make the first move.

journal prompt

What do you enjoy doing physically, I mean actually enjoy? There are a lot of things you should enjoy, or you pretend to enjoy, but what moves your body and makes you feel good?

Put a check next to any of the items below that you enjoy:

- ___ walking
- ___ having sex
- ___ dancing
- ___ jogging
- ___ aerobics
- ___ CrossFit
- ___ swimming
- ___ stretching
- ___ boxing
- ___ biking
- ___ Pilates
- ___ yoga
- ___ biking
- ___ competitive team sports
- ___ Zumba

What can you do to make one of these activities possible in your life? Make a plan to do it this week.

YOUR BODY IS A GIFT. OUR BODIES AND SPIRITS ARE INTIMATELY CONNECTED. THE MORE WE RESPECT OUR BODIES, THE BETTER WE CAN CARE FOR OTHERS.

FIVE.

TO WORK
- or -
NOT TO
WORK
and what to do all day

intention:

THE GOAL OF THIS CHAPTER IS TO HELP YOU ORGANIZE AND BALANCE YOUR HOME LIFE AND PROFESSIONAL LIFE.

THE DECISION OF HOW TO BALANCE YOUR TIME AND ENERGY IN A FAMILY UNIT IS A SACRED, PERSONAL DECISION.

Ahh, to work or not to work…as a mama in the twenty-first century that is the ultimate question! One marvelous thing about our generation is that women, for the first time in history, are presented with dozens of options for full-time, flextime, part-time, or from-home work. Although we still have far to go, our generation enjoys the greatest opportunities for women, and their families—as we work our way toward gender equality in the workplace and better childcare options. But with innovation and progression also come a new slew of challenges. To me, the challenge for the twenty-first century mom looks like this:

1. SHOULD I BE PURSUING A CAREER OUTSIDE OF BEING A MOM AND A HOMEMAKER?

2. HOW DO I IMPLEMENT BALANCE IN EITHER SITUATION?

I started my journey as a mom intending to have a large family and not work outside of the home. As our family has evolved, things have changed, and I have found myself in every single working scenario. Since having kids, I have been a: full-time stay-at-home mom; stay-at-home working mom; mom full-time in an office; and now co-parenting, co-officing mom. (I bet you didn't even know those existed. ME NEITHER.) The point is that your situation will change as your family progresses, but whatever stage you're in right now, there is something right for you and your work-home-life balance. The goal is to find what that is.

The decision of how to balance your time and energy in a family unit is a sacred, personal decision. We spend a lot of time thinking about our financial bank accounts, but we also have a "time bank account," with a certain amount of time and energy in each day. I would argue that where we allocate the funds of our time bank account is even more important than how we allocate our actual finances. When one partner in a marriage

there is something right for you.

has a health issue or a career that demands more time and energy, often the other partner has to scale back his or her professional goals. This can be really challenging—especially when you are trying to factor in your little one's' best interest. I hope these activities help you come to terms with your current situation. And let us all remember one thing—taking care of your child IS A FULL-TIME JOB. So, whatever you decide to do—or not do—just remember you are already performing the most important calling and duty anyone can perform—caring for a baby. After staying at home, working from home, and working out of the home, I have learned one thing: I would NEVER tell another woman what I think she should do with her professional life after starting a family. We've already established that the most important thing a child needs is a happy, healthy, you—and what you spend your day doing will be a large part of how you find that happiness.

Wishing you all of the luck in your journey, Mama.

xx
Andrea

"IT IS IMPOSSIBLE TO WIN THE GREAT PRIZES OF LIFE WITHOUT RUNNING RISKS, AND THE GREATEST OF ALL PRIZES ARE THOSE CONNECTED WITH THE HOME."

THEODORE ROOSEVELT

WHAT IS YOUR CURRENT LIFE SITUATION? WHO IS MAKING THE MONEY AND WHO IS WATCHING THE KIDS?	WHAT'S YOUR IDEAL LIFE SITUATION? WHO WOULD BE MAKING THE MONEY? WHO WOULD BE WATCHING THE KIDS? WHAT KIND OF WORK WOULD EACH OF YOU BE DOING?

WHAT ARE 4 THINGS STOPPING YOU FROM TURNING YOUR CURRENT SITUATION INTO YOUR DREAM?

journal prompt

LET'S EXAMINE ANY LIMITING BELIEFS YOU MIGHT HAVE.

TAKE THE LIST OF 4 THINGS FROM THE PREVIOUS PAGE AND WRITE A SOLUTION FOR 3 OF THEM BELOW.

For example, "No childcare. Solution: Trade babysitting days with friends, work in the evenings when baby is in bed, hire a babysitter two days a week."

Take your remaining limitations and honestly sort through your fears, assumptions, and reality to take the reins on what you *can* control.

MAMA tips

FIND A MENTOR

Seek out women in a similar situation. Find mentors, or women you admire—they might be women who have chosen to stay home or women who lead companies. Do everything in your power to look outside of your limiting beliefs.

FAVORITE RESOURCES

LEAN IN
by Sheryl Sandberg

GIFTS OF IMPERFECTION
by Brene Brown

BIG MAGIC
by Elizabeth Gilbert

HOW I BUILT THIS
Podcast by NPR

VISUALIZATION ACITIVITY

STRIKE A BALANCE

Here's what a perfect schedule would look like. Draw where you'd be in a perfect world.

THESE THINGS FILL ME UP	THESE THINGS DRAIN ME

journal prompt

PICTURE YOURSELF AT 70

What is meaningful and motivating to one woman might be dramatically different from what is meaningful and motivating to another. Picture yourself at 70 years old, about to go to brunch with friends on a sunny spring day. As you're talking to girlfriends at brunch, what types of experiences are you reminiscing about? What makes you feel proud? What accomplishments feel noteworthy to you? You will not wake up tomorrow and be 70, but one day you will. Think about one thing you would like to see in your life at that point, and write it below:

SELF-ANALYSIS QUIZ

MAKE A CHECK MARK NEXT TO EVERYTHING THAT APPLIES TO YOU:

___ Working outside the home (or the idea of it) gives me a sense of peace.

___ Working outside the home (or the idea of it) doesn't seem like a choice.

___ I am happier when I have a lot on my plate and bounce from activity to activity.

___ I am happier when I have time to move through my day without having to feel rushed.

___ Assuming I had one million dollars in the bank, there are still careers I would want to pursue.

___ Motherhood is very fulfilling to me, and I don't spend a lot of time looking elsewhere for satisfaction.

___ I often feel that the choices I have made regarding work are right for this season of my life.

___ I spend a lot of time questioning whether I am spending my time and resources wisely.

BELIEVE THAT YOU'LL KNOW WHAT'S BEST AT EVERY SEASON IN YOUR LIFE.

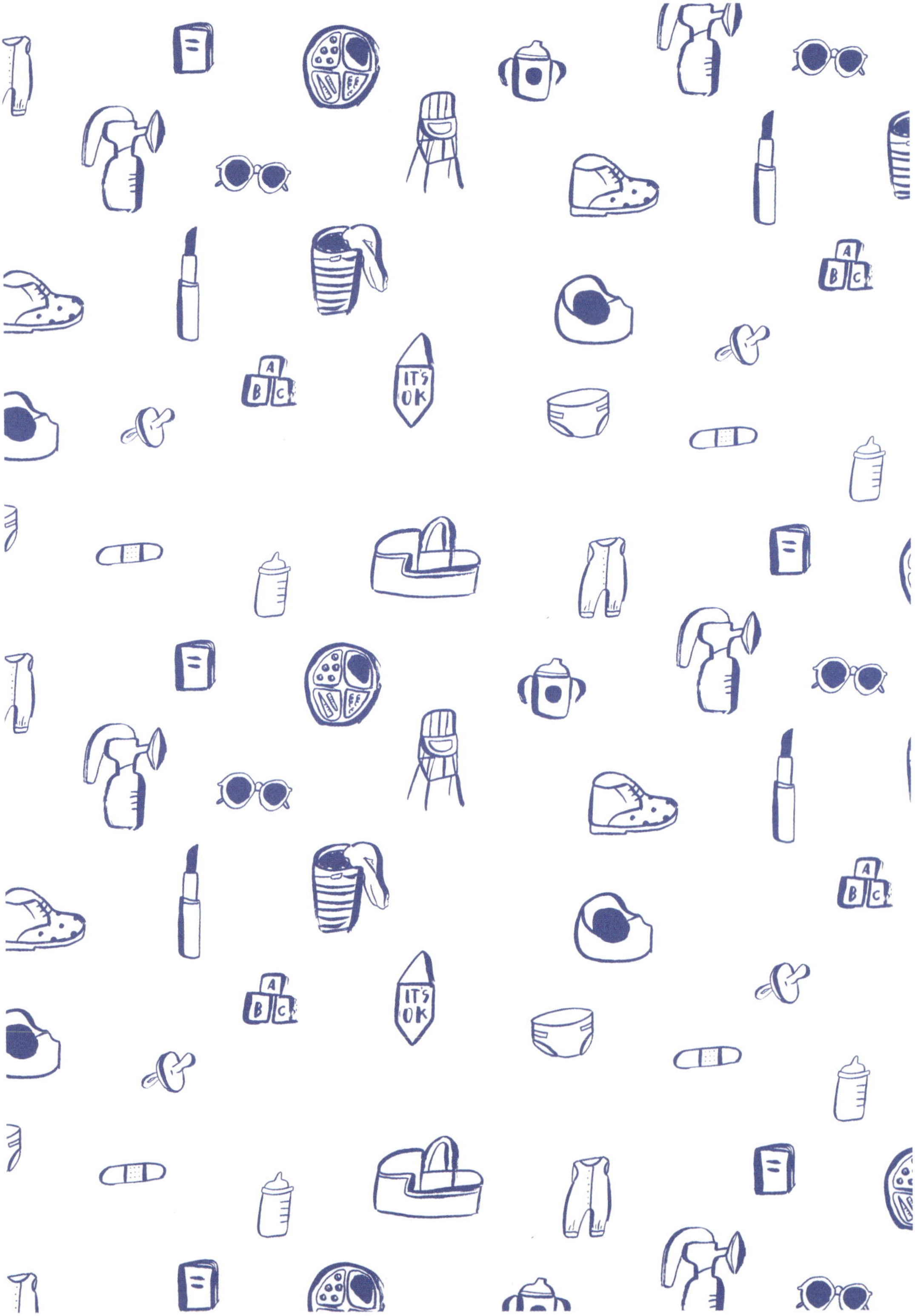
IT'S OK
IT'S OK

SIX.

There's No Place like Home

intention:

THE GOAL OF THIS CHAPTER IS TO THINK ABOUT YOUR "HOME CULTURE" AND HOW YOU CAN MAKE IT WHAT YOU WANT.

TO ME, CREATING A COZY HOME IS LIKE ANYTHING ELSE—IT STARTS WITH DECIDING WHAT YOU VALUE AND SETTING PRIORITIES.

Sometimes while aimlessly scrolling through Instagram (which I'm sure you never do…) I come across images of a baby's nursery, completely finished, sometimes weeks before the child's arrival. I am talking, clothes washed and folded, pictures hung on walls, and stuffed animals lined up in the crib, just waiting for that little one to arrive. And each time I see those pictures I think, "HOW IS THAT EVEN POSSIBLE?!" I am struggling along here, celebrating every single load of laundry I complete, and you're over there with your gallery walls, blowing me away! I am also hoping one of these high efficiency mamas will, very soon, come hang all of the frames I have stacked in each room of my home. (Let me know if you're the girl for the job.)

I'm three babies into this mothering gig and I have yet to bring a baby home to a completed nursery. So, in a way, I feel slightly sheepish about giving anyone advice about "making a house a home," but I would argue that each mother will have strengths to demonstrate in her homemaking efforts. Because when I say "homemaking" I'm talking about the literal making of a home: not ruffly aprons or canning peaches. When I talk about "homemaking" I'm referring to the painstaking, day-after-day, love-filled venture of turning a house into a warm, comfortable, safe place you'd want to be in more than anywhere in the world. I'm not an interior decorator or feng shui guru, but I do love a home that reflects the family that lives in it. To me, homemaking isn't about decorating with fake ferns above your kitchen cabinets, or even having the newest, hippest, mid-century modern furniture—it's about taking responsibility for the culture you're creating every day in your home.

To me, creating a cozy home is like anything else—it starts with deciding what you value and setting priorities. Food has always been my love language and a favorite way of mine to share love with those close to me. Between our business and our little ones' schedules, it feels challenging to eat a sit-down family dinner every night. Our family meals during the week are typically fast, efficient, and I rarely have a second to do anything but attend to everyone's needs. But every Sunday I cook and we set the table, and we all sit down together and talk. We eat slowly. I prepare all week for what I'm going to make for our family Sunday dinner. It is one of my children's favorite traditions.

I do love a home that reflects the family who lives in it.

Another home ritual that is extremely important to us is bath time. (I know, I know… what did you think I was going to say?) We make it long and fun, and the whole family is involved. Every Monday night we have a set-aside family planning session and game night. On Fridays we typically watch a movie together. I guess what I'm trying to say is that when it comes to homemaking, there are so many things I DON'T do, but there a few things that Brian and I have made a priority, and that is how we've created our home. Those things, far more than the surface look, make it our special place.

I hope in this chapter you feel encouraged to embrace the parts of homemaking that come naturally to you. And can we make a group decision to drop the things we aren't shining at and hope that our kids will be able to take those as an elective one day in high school? Sound like a plan? Alright great. I'm in. You're doing an incredible job, Mama.

xx
Andrea

Goodnight stars.

Goodnight air.

Goodnight noises everywhere.

MARGARET WISE BROWN
GOODNIGHT MOON

SELF-ANALYSIS QUIZ

Answer each question as thoughts come to your mind.

_____ is a place I feel really happy.

I hate going to _____ because it feels
_____

I love the smell of _____

One thing my child does that I always find funny is _____
_____
_____

I feel the calmest when I'm _____
_____
_____

I feel uneasy when I am _____
_____
_____

Something I do everyday to make our home wonderful is _____
_____
_____

Something I wish I did everyday in our home is _____
_____
_____

EMBRACE HYGGE

In Denmark, there's a Danish word for making your living space warm, inviting, cozy, and comfortable. It's called "Hygge" (pronounced hoo-gah). It's an integral part of Danish culture, evolving from their long, harsh winters. It's all about using soft materials, like fuzzy knitted socks and blankets; bringing in multiple lamps for soft lighting; serving warm drinks; and bringing loved ones together. Embrace it.

VISUALIZATION ACITIVITY

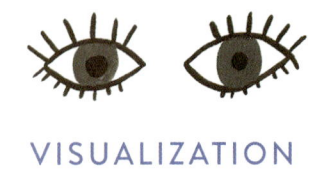

~~DO IT ALL~~ AS MUCH AS YOU CAN

LIST 10 HOUSEHOLD ACTIVITIES THAT ARE OVERWHELMING YOU

LIST A WAY TO SIMPLIFY THE ACTIVITIES IN COLUMN #1

For example: ask for help, schedule time to get it done, put less pressure to do things that might not be 100% necessary (like making elaborate homemade meals every night).

VISUALIZATION ACITIVITY

TRADITIONS MAKE HOME LIFE FUN

THERE ARE FEW THINGS IN LIFE I LOOK FORWARD TO MORE THAN _____,
_____,
AND _____.
GROWING UP, I LOVED THAT MY FAMILY _____
_____.

HERE ARE A FEW TRADITIONS I HOPE TO SHARE WITH MY FAMILY IN MY OWN HOME: _____,
_____,
_____,
_____,
_____.

**ADD 5 TRADITIONS
YOU HOPE TO INCORPORATE INTO
YOUR FAMILY THIS NEXT YEAR.**

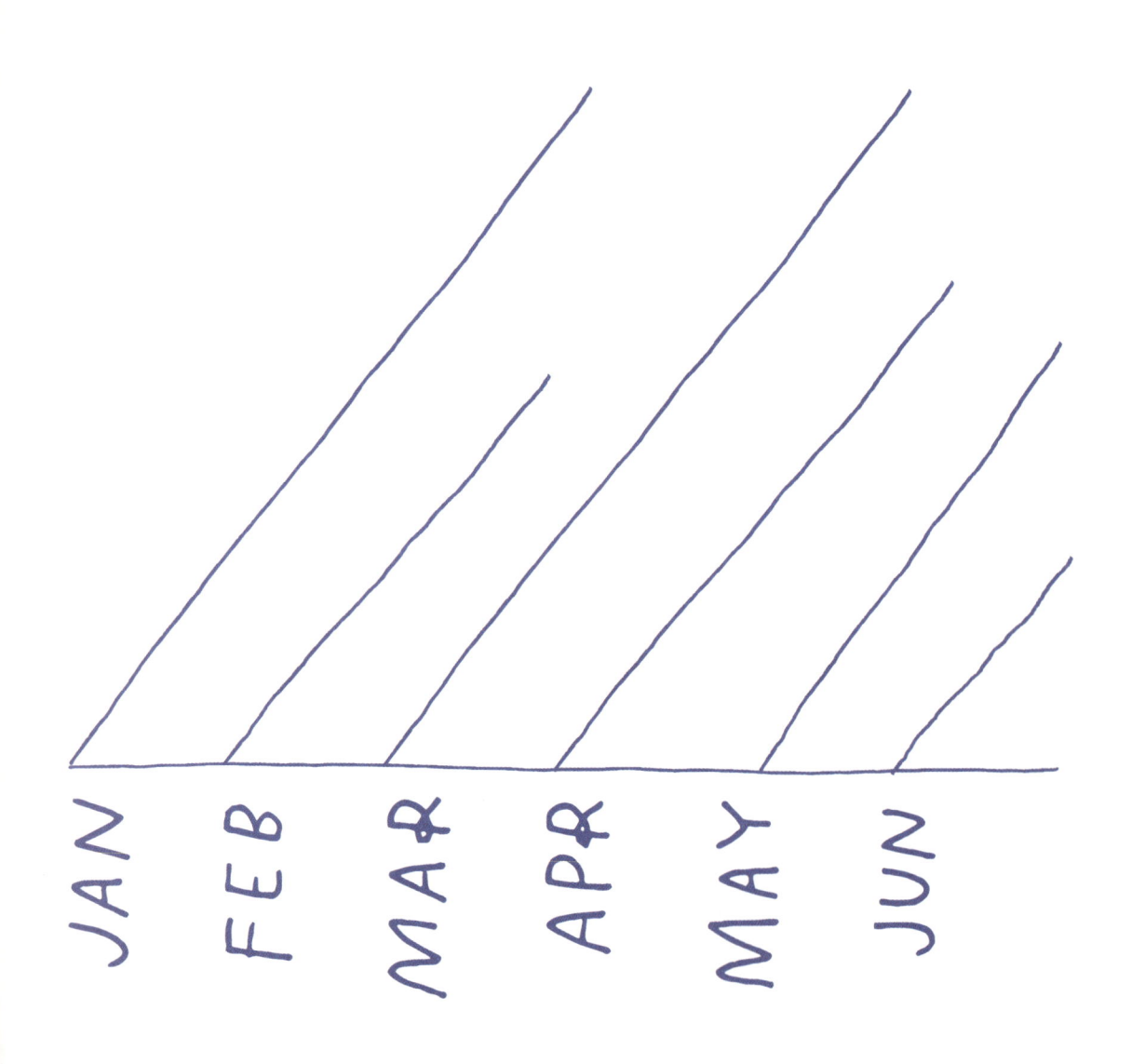

| JAN | FEB | MAR | APR | MAY | JUN |

JUL AUG SEP OCT NOV DEC

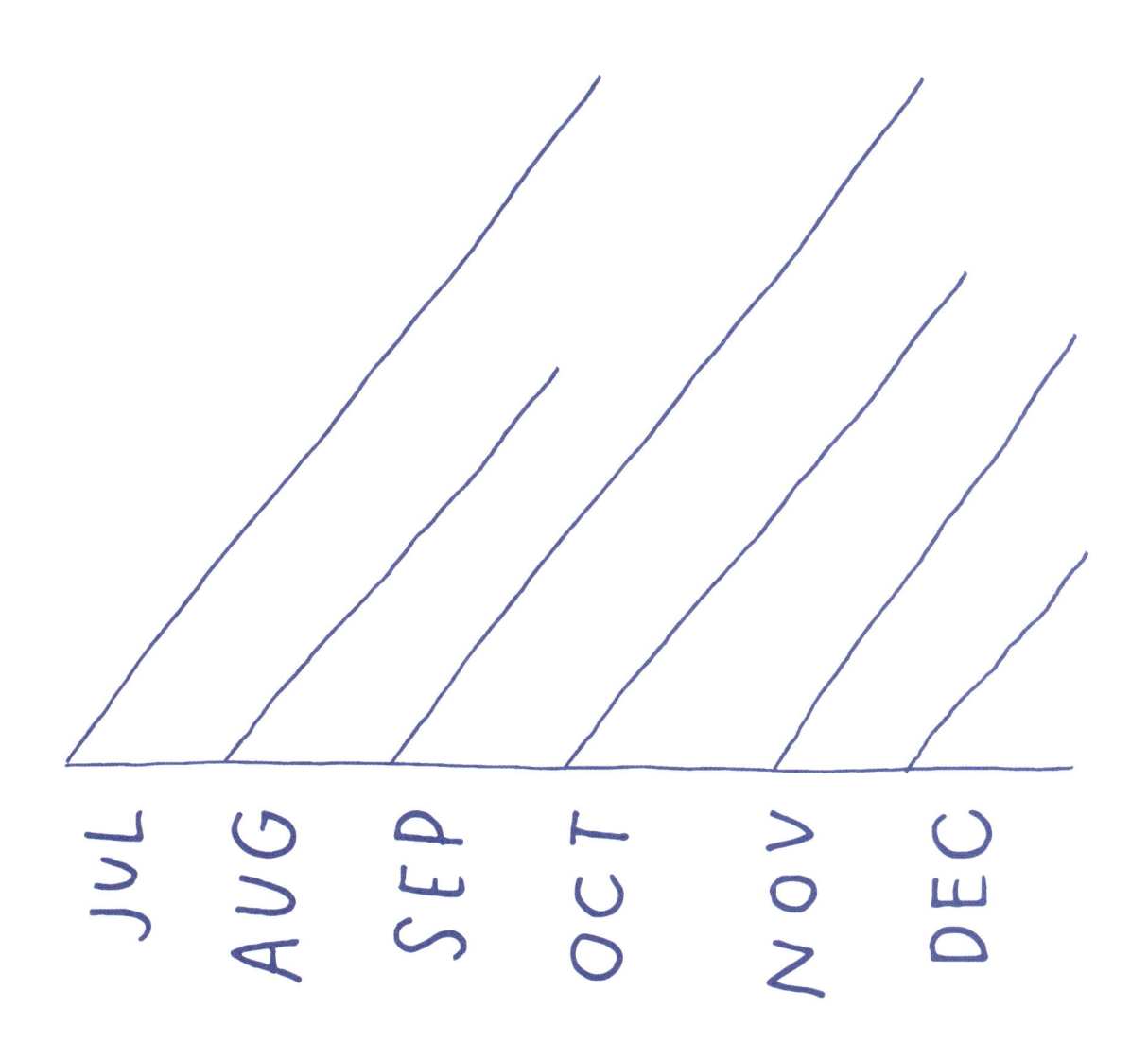

Where Thou Art — that is Home.

EMILY DICKINSON

FAMILY NIGHT

Choose one night a week to hang out together and have fun. My family does something called "Family Home Evening." It's a Mormon family tradition that started in the '70s. Every Monday night (or whatever night works best), we gather together and make it all about our family. We sing a children's hymn together, say a prayer (it's a great way to teach your kids to pray out loud), read a few scripture verses, and have a very short lesson on a theme like "sharing" or "gratitude." I love the feeling that fills our home as we spend this time together. Our kids are really little, so we never really know how it's going to go, but even if everything falls apart, I'm still proud of us for trying! We usually play Candy Land and eat some ice cream too. (Gotta have a treat!)

Circle some activities you would like to do together as a family:

- (Christmas Day Breakfast)
- Write a Family Motto or Manifesto
- Date nights w/ your kids (one parent takes one child out alone)
- Birthday present search (a scavenger hunt for birthday presents)
- Perform service together the week of Christmas
- Easter baskets
- Family recipe book
- Writing birthday messages in books you give
- Summer vacations
- Cheese soiree on Christmas Eve
- Homemade chili and trick-or-treating with friends on Halloween night
- Weed together every Saturday morning
- Drive-in movie at the end of summer
- Camp together
- Eat tacos on the beach at sunset
- Make mom breakfast in bed on Mother's Day
- Make family movies every year
- Friday Date Night

Sing at the top of your lungs together on road trips

Get new pajamas on Christmas Eve

Make a family picture gallery wall

Choose a "Family Theme Song" every year

Make Family Goals every year on January 1

Junk Cereal Fridays

Read stories every night before bed

Make Dad breakfast in bed on Father's Day

Give a hug and a kiss when greeting each other (Let your kids see!)

Say "I love you" when saying goodbye or when hanging up the phone

Family prayer before you leave the house in the morning

Regular Family Counsel: anybody can ask a question or make a suggestion

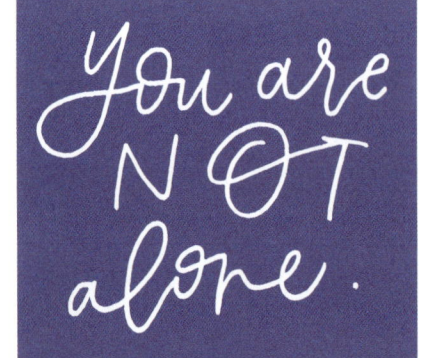

You are NOT alone.

Psychologist Marshal Duke has found that children who have an intimate knowledge of their family's history are typically more well-adjusted and self-confident than children who don't. There's something about understanding your past and knowing you belong to something bigger than yourself that instills confidence. Tell your kids how you and your partner met, and don't leave out any funny details. Tell them about your first apartment, your crappy car, trying to find your first real job in a big city. It gives kids something to turn to during hard times: if they've heard stories about how you've gotten through hard things before, they're more likely to believe they can do it as well.

simplify,
simplify,
simplify.

HENRY DAVID
THOREAU

journal prompt

There is a lot that happens in our homes that we cannot control. (I cannot control how many times my children pull every blanket we own into the family room to build a fort, for example.) But I can control a few things. Think of the things around your home you do have control over. What does it smell like? Could you add a favorite candle, or open windows more often? What music is playing? Is the TV on too often? Are there shoes scattered everywhere that could be placed in a bin? Pause and work through the things you can control—what simple elements can you add to your home so it will be a place both you and your little ones love to be.

YOU HAVE THE POWER TO CREATE THE HOME YOU WANT FOR YOUR CHILDREN.

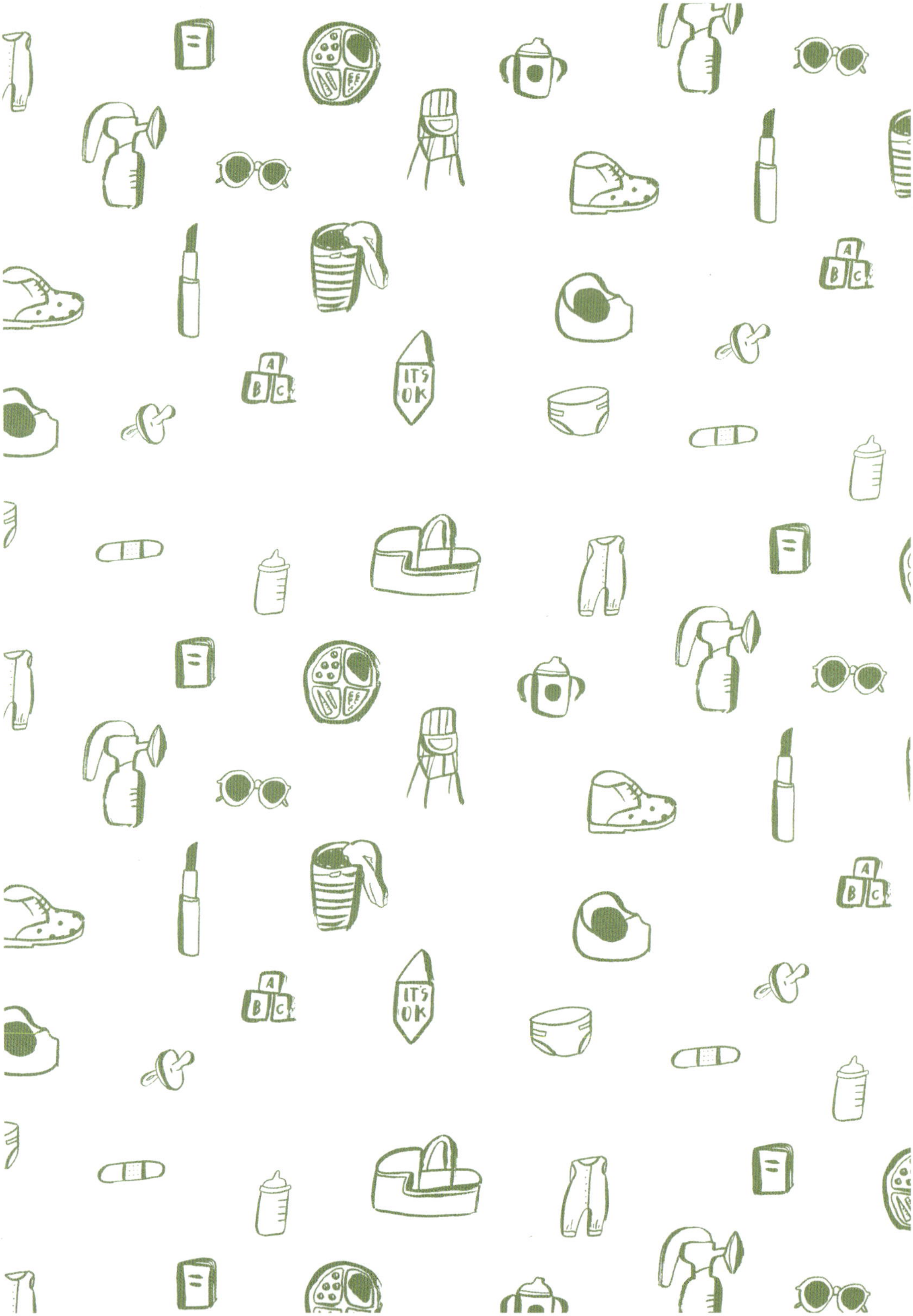
IT'S OK
IT'S OK

SEVEN.

Keep the END in MIND

intention:

THE GOAL OF THIS CHAPTER IS TO HELP YOU PRIORITIZE YOUR SPIRITUAL AND EMOTIONAL HEALTH.

WHAT MAKES ME, ME IS WHERE I SHOULD BE SPENDING MY TIME EVERY DAY; IT IS HOW I AM ABLE TO BE MY BEST SELF.

Sometimes I can't remember what really makes me happy, what I really want to accomplish in life, and what I'm working towards. I mean, I'm a mom, wife, business owner, and so you'd think those titles would be enough to keep me satisfied, but sometimes during the day-to-day quiet moments, I start to feel crazy like, "What am I doing with my life?" Do you ever do that? As a mom or caretaker, it is easy to have these moments when you question yourself because your life is so much less structured than it was in a corporate or scholastic setting. No grades, no performance reviews, no boss looking over your shoulder saying, "Good work!" It's hard to know how to measure your success.

So, in moments of uncertainty, this is what I do . . . are you ready? I imagine my funeral! Gruesome, right? Just hang with me. I think, "What would I want people to say about me at my funeral? Who would I want there? What do I want it to feel like?" Asking these questions reminds me what I really value, because when all is said and done, I value some things more than others and those are the things that make me, ME. And what makes me, ME is where I should be spending my time every day; it is how I am able to be my best self.

So now you want to know what my funeral will be like, don't you? (Or what I hope it will be like . . . And yes, you are totally invited.) This whole "live like you want your funeral to be like" idea came to me after attending my great-aunt Leola Green Merrill's funeral while I was a sophomore in college. She had four very accomplished kids, and a huge group of grandchildren who were darling, well-dressed, educated, and well-spoken. At her funeral, the church was packed with people who loved Leola and remembered her for her outspoken wit and her dedication to the arts, her faith, and family. They remembered the loving things she did and said, such as how she would call people at church when they got a new assignment to tell them how great they would be. Darling, right? Or how she would invite the neighborhood kids over to rehearse their speaking parts for church programs. People also mentioned things like what a fabulous public speaker she was and how in love she and her husband were.

"I don't even know who I am!"

I decided right then that I wanted a funeral just like Leola's, so I better start living in a way that would help me be the type of person who leaves a legacy like hers. So when I feel like, "I don't even know who I am!" I think of my funeral and I ask, "Am I a woman who reaches out to my local community on a level that is meaningful to them? Am I a committed wife and mom? Do I use my talents in a way that helps benefit others?" And most importantly, "Am I living every single day to develop the attributes I want my family to remember me for?" I'm reminded that the things I work on every day will make me the person I want to become.

Do you ever struggle knowing where to place your energy as a mom? I hope in this chapter you find the tools to help you emotionally and spiritually progress while you are taking care of your little ones.

xx
Andrea

HAPPINESS

IS NEITHER VIRTUE

NOR PLEASURE

NOR THIS THING

NOR THAT,

BUT SIMPLE GROWTH.

We are happy when we are growing.

WILLIAM BUTLER YEATS

RESEARCH HAS ESTABLISHED A SUBSTANTIAL LINK BETWEEN MOTHERS WHO FEEL DEPRESSED AND "NEGATIVE OUTCOMES" IN THEIR CHILDREN. ONE STUDY FOUND THAT *happy parents are statistically more likely to have happy children.*

Source: http://time.com/35496/how-to-raise-happy-kids-10-steps-backed-by-science/

SELF-ANALYSIS QUIZ:
FIND SATISFACTION IN YOUR OWN LIFE

What is the best way to show more love to your little ones? Find satisfaction in your own life. Deep, emotional, soul-smacking satisfaction. I'm not saying your life has to be perfect, or you have to love your job, or be totally happy with the way every color coded jar is lined up in your pantry. I'm saying it's up to you to do the work to be happy with your life. That could mean going to therapy. That could mean getting a job. That could mean leaving your job to be at home. That could mean moving to a smaller house or having three more kids or saying no to someone you've never said no to before. Or it could mean making other really tough, life-altering decisions.

How am I doing?

	Never	Hardly Ever	Some Days	Totally!
Are you satisfied with your life right now?	O	O	O	O
Do you make your emotional health a priority in your life?	O	O	O	O
When necessary do you seek help (professional help, help from partner, help from friends)?	O	O	O	O
Do you believe your emotional well being is as important as caring for your children?	O	O	O	O
Do you make time to be still and have some "me" time every single day?	O	O	O	O
Are you always looking for ways to progress spiritually?	O	O	O	O

Reject your sense of injury and the injury itself disappears.

MARCUS AURELIUS

QUIET RECHARGE

Find time every single day to recharge yourself spiritually. Set the goal to do this every day for a week for just 10 minutes, and then adjust the time as you feel you need it.

YOU MIGHT:

Write in a journal
Meditate formally on a mat
Spend time in prayer
Spend time reading scripture

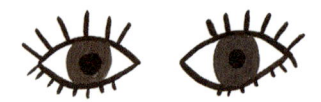

VISUALIZATION ACITIVTY

Get down on your knees to pray or close your eyes to begin meditating. What are the things you focus on? Using symbols, stick figures, detailed depictions, or words, draw or write what you pray for or meditate on in the thought bubbles below.

What do you have gratitude for right now?

What goals do you have for your meditation today?
(Calmness, strength, love, etc.)

What three questions do you need direction on in your life?

FAVORITE RESOURCES

BOLD NEW MOM
A podcast that encourages emotional strength by Jody Moore

DARING GREATLY
by Brene Brown

10% HAPPIER WITH DAN HARRIS.
A podcast featuring various people and how they incorporate mindfulness

BLESSED IS SHE
A religious journal to record thoughts and prayer
www.blessedisshe.net

REVISITING YOUR PREVIOUS JOURNAL PROMPTS IN THIS BOOK

SELF-ANALYSIS QUIZ

1. Draw a bubble cloud around 3 words that describe how you felt today:

OVERWHELMED	SAD	MEAN
GRATEFUL	TIRED	LAZY
JEALOUS	LOVING	PEACEFUL
TENSE	CONTENT	CRUMMY
JOYFUL	FRANTIC	WORRIED
MOODY	CALM	LIKE A BOSS
HOPEFUL	TALKATIVE	CONFUSED

2. Choose a word that describes the way you *want* to feel and write it in beautiful handwriting below:

3. Underline all the phrases you agree with:

I did something meaningful for someone else today.

I took a moment for myself today.

I have someone I look up to.

I thought about or prayed for someone else today.

I do at least one thing each day that I enjoy.

I seek out advice and try and listen.

I can think of one thing I am really good at.

I feel in control of my emotions most of the time.

journal prompt

What do you hope most for your little ones? What attributes would you most like them to develop? Do you hope they feel their divine potential? Do you feel that for yourself? How are you working to develop the same attributes you hope they will one day possess?

KEEP THE END IN MIND WHEN SETTING PRIORITIES FOR YOURSELF.

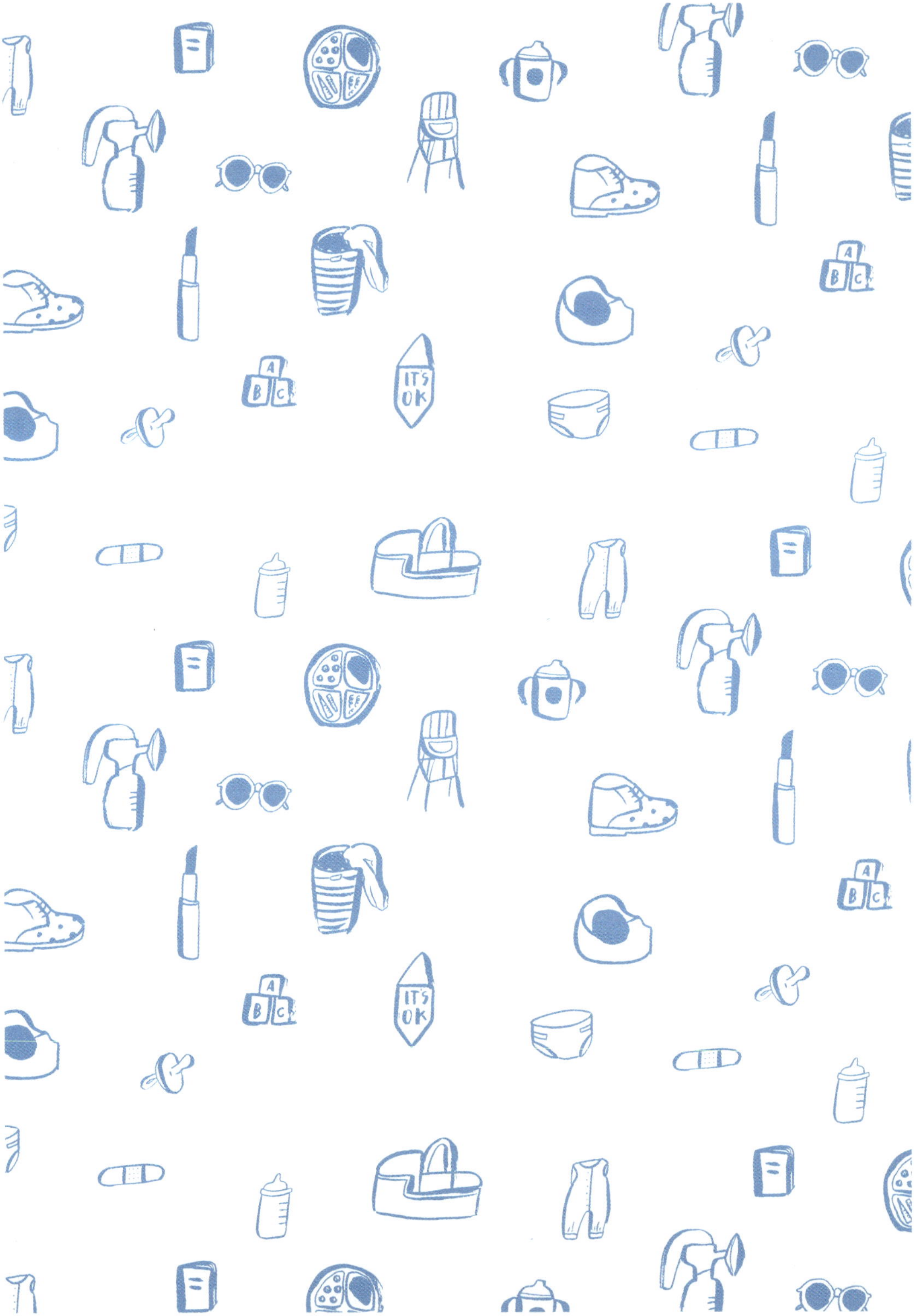
IT'S OK

EIGHT.

HOW TO BUILD A VILLAGE

intention:

THE GOAL FOR THIS CHAPTER IS TO RECOGNIZE YOUR NEED FOR A VILLAGE WHILE YOU RAISE YOUR LITTLE ONES.

I HAVE WORKED HARD TO CULTIVATE A VILLAGE WITH WHICH WE CAN RAISE OUR FAMILY.

A few months ago, I was at the gym picking my kids up from daycare. A woman I've talked with a few times while on the treadmill came in to pick up her son after being called on the intercom. She was in the middle of potty training him and during his time in daycare he had taken his pants down and peed in the corner of the gym play place. (Every mom's nightmare, right?) When she came to pick him up she rushed him into the bathroom. She looked calm and wasn't embarrassed, but I knew that it wasn't her finest moment either. As parents, our days sometimes feel defined by the actions of these little people we care for. How early our kids learn to talk, walk, potty train, or ride a bike somehow becomes a ruler for measuring our success as a parent. In reality, we should not measure our performance by their successes or failures, but more by the way we love and care for them as they hit (or maybe miss?) these milestones at their own pace.

I left the gym without talking to that mom and felt sorry for the rest of the day. I should have waited and said something to lighten the mood like, "One time when I was potty training my little girl she peed all over my huge pregnant belly in Target." Or I could have shared the time when I had just had a baby and I peed all over myself when I tried to jump with my kids in a bounce house! Or I could even have just said something as simple as, "Those first few days out of the house while potty training are the WORST!" (Because they are!)

Whatever it was I could have said, I know I should have said something, because as parents of young children, we are all in this together. If we don't reach out to one another to empathize when our kids pee on the floor, then all we have left—literally—is stinky kids and a puddle of pee. We don't have to expose our worst flaws to make someone feel better, but it never hurts to say, "I totally know how that feels!" No one will ever be offended. In fact, they will probably feel validated and understood. I have always been

We are all in this together.

a social person, and loved having a network of friends. But as I have had children, I have come to need more and more support in my life.

I am a part of online groups (like the Tubby Todd Mama Facebook Group and those I follow on social media.) I have a network of friends in my neighborhood that I carpool with, I have my coworkers, my church friends, my family, and my gal pals. I am one blessed individual. But I haven't always had lots of friends to interact with. Becoming a mom can be isolating and involves changes that are sometimes out of your control. I have had a lot of lonely days when I wished I had something fun to look forward to, or a friend to meet up with. So I have worked hard to cultivate a village with which we can raise our family. From these women I have learned how to be a mom. I have learned "mom hacks" that have helped me hang onto my sanity during my darkest days. Both my children and I love lunch dates and park dates. My social network, my village, is what makes family life fun and inspiring.

xx
Andrea

If we can share our story with someone who responds with empathy and understanding, SHAME can't SURVIVE.

BRENE BROWN
DARING GREATLY

IF YOU HAVE GOOD

THOUGHTS THEY WILL

SHINE OUT OF YOUR FACE

LIKE SUNBEAMS

you will always look lovely,

ROALD DAHL

journal prompt

WHO IS YOUR BEST FRIEND?

WHAT SPECIAL QUALITIES DOES THAT PERSON POSSESS?

WHO IS A MOM YOU ADMIRE?

WHAT IS IT ABOUT THIS PERSON THAT DRAWS YOU TO HER?

WHAT CAN YOU LEARN FROM HER EXAMPLE AS A MAMA?

VISUALIZATION ACITIVITY

INTROVERT, EXTROVERT, OR BOTH: IT'S GOOD TO GET OUT

Schedule time to see another adult every single day. I would love to say that I can go days and days with only the company of my little ones, but the reality is, I can't! In fact, I've realized I probably shouldn't go even one day without having some real adult conversation. Fill in the calendar below with the times and people you will see for the next seven days.

DAY 1	DAY 2
DAY 3	DAY 4
DAY 5	DAY 6
DAY 7	

MAMA WHO KNOWS

There's just nothing like having a tribe of women around you who know exactly what you are going through. That's why having so-called 'mom friends' is so key. When I was 7 months pregnant with my son, I only knew one or two other women from my local creative community who were also raising children. I really looked to them as an example of being able to do both—have children and have interesting careers and lives. Because we were hungry to find more mothers that fit this mold and that we could relate to as women, my friend Jeanne Chan and I started what we jokingly dubbed the 'Cool Moms Club' with a Facebook group of the same name. We added friends and acquaintances who then added their friends and acquaintances, and now five years later, we have an incredible local moms club with nearly 500 fantastic women in it (and a 100+ person waitlist)!

The power of this community cannot be understated. I've met some of my very best friends through this group, and we've all become lifelines for each other's sanity, happiness, and career mentorship. Many of our kids are now great buddies, but the magic is that as adults we're connecting on a level that goes beyond motherhood—and many of us would be friends even if we didn't have littles. The fact that we are juggling children at the same time as doing everything else in our lives is really what makes our bonds extra-strong. I've also seen several of the women in this group be inspired by each other's entrepreneurial pursuits and start businesses as a response to the club and the framework of support it provides. It's honestly one of the reasons so many of us don't want to move away from the Bay Area, because we've found our people.

KATIE Hintz-Zambrano

Katie Hintz-Zambrano is the co-founder of mothermag.com and the creator of Be in Good Company, a conference for creative, entrepreneurial mothers. Katie founded mothermag.com after having her first child — a son, Diego — in April 2013. She noticed a gaping hole in the market for a full-service, style-leaning parenting site. Kaite lives with her husband and Diego in San Francisco, CA.

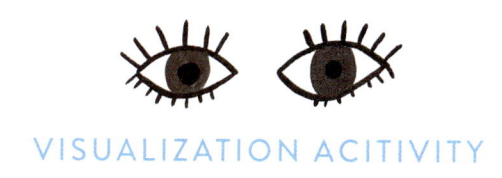

VISUALIZATION ACITIVITY
HOW TO MAKE MOM FRIENDS

Everybody wants to know how to make "mom friends," right?! I don't think there's some big secret, but I do know it takes work and getting out of yourself. If you're willing to reach out, you'll find your village. Here is the equation:

ONE MOM FRIEND YOU REALLY LIKE + YOUR KIDS GET ALONG = HAPPY VILLAGE.

Sometimes making new mom friends can feel like the first day of high school! If you're feeling awkward or dumb about picking up on a mom, here's a 'lil sample convo for you:

You slyly approach a mom nearby who's playing with her daughter in the sandbox.

YOU: She's so cute! How old is your daughter?

HER: Thanks. 18 months.

Pause.

YOU: Oh awesome. My son is 18 months too. Is your daughter still putting everything in her mouth like my son is?

HER: Yeah! Ha ha. I have to watch her all the time.

YOU: Ha ha. Oh, I forgot to introduce myself. I'm _____. And you're…? Do you live nearby?

HER: My name is _____. I do live nearby. Just one street over.

YOU: We love to get out and go to parks. Let me get your number and if we're here, we'll text you so we can meet up. Maybe we could have a picnic sometime?

See, that's not so bad. It's good to remember that you've got nothing to lose. Only awesome mom friends to gain!

You are NOT alone.

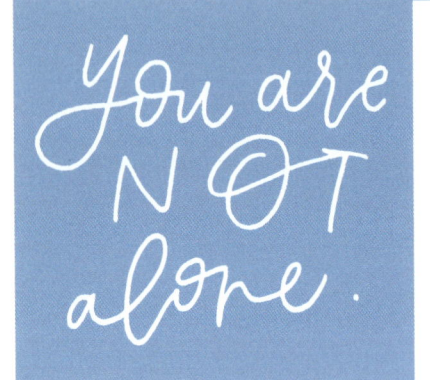

"We were looking for a home to rent and had just had what seemed like our 20th showing. I felt like this house might be the one. We had just moved across the country, and I was super nervous and stressed—everything felt too new. I was buckling my two kids into the car when a mom walking by stopped and said Hi and I said Hi and mentioned we were maybe moving in that house. She congratulated me, asked if she could give me her number, and raved about the neighborhood. She introduced her adorable girls, waved goodbye, and went on her way, but I was never the same. Her friendliness meant more than she would ever know."

— NOT UNCOMMON LONELY MOM

SELF-ANALYSIS QUIZ

1= NEVER
2= SOMETIMES
3= OFTEN
4= ALMOST ALWAYS
5= ALWAYS

_____ I invite people over for dinner at least once a month.

_____ I ask for people's help or advice when I'm faced with something particularly challenging.

_____ I feel there are people in my life I could send a cute picture of my child to.

_____ I reach out to others when I think they may be struggling.

_____ I look for ways to strengthen the friendships I have in my life and try to be a good friend.

_____ I include others in social settings where groups are involved.

MAMA *tips*

BUILDING A VILLAGE TAKES RESILIENCE

Don't let the PARADE pass you by.

If you desperately need that village and you're not finding it, DON'T GIVE UP. I promise you—friends are out there. Don't leave one Internet forum, Facebook mom group, parenting app, MeetUp, neighborhood playground, church play group, or library storytime untried. They're waiting for you, too. You'll find them.

FAVORITE RESOURCES

HOW TO FIND MOM FRIENDS

Tubby Todd Mama Group (you can set up a mom meetup in your city)

Meetup.com

Hellomamas.com

Peanuts

SmartMom

Mush

Winnie

Parenthoods app

What to Expect app

MomLife app

https://mom.life/

Mom blogs

Start your own blog

Neighborhood playground

Library storytimes

MOPS (Mothers of Preschoolers) http://www.mops.org/

Toy aisle at Target

Church, non-denominational, neighborhood playgroups

Public pools

Swim lessons

Preschool

Introductions through other friends

Indoor play spaces

Soccer practice

YMCA kid's activities

Neighborhood block parties

Go trick-or-treating and meet your neighbors. Introduce yourselves and say you'd love to get together sometime.

Conferences, getaways, overnighters

journal prompt

Think of a friendship you admire. This can come from a friend's life, TV show, book, movie, or your life.

Wait, pause. Really think of a relationship before continuing.

What about this relationship do you admire?

Do you think you are anything like either of the people in the relationship?

Do you think you are capable of a relationship like this?

Now think of a person you would like to have a better relationship with. What small, manageable steps could you take to get on that path? Let's get you started... could you send them light-hearted texts to get a conversation going? Send them something small in the mail? Ask them for advice on something they are good at? Don't overwhelm yourself, just think of one person and one thing that might help strengthen your relationship. We build our villages one person at a time.

WE'RE BETTER TOGETHER.
YOU DON'T HAVE TO DO THIS ALONE.
REACH OUT AND BUILD THE MOTHERLY CIRCLE
OF SUPPORT THAT YOU NEED.

Before You Go

EVERYTHING YOUR CHILD NEEDS LIVES WITHIN YOU.

MAKE TIME EVERYDAY TO CARE FOR YOURSELF.

MOTHERHOOD IS FULL OF EVER-CHANGING SEASONS.

STRONG WOMEN KNOW WHEN TO ASK FOR HELP.

THE MORE WE RESPECT OUR BODIES,
THE BETTER WE CAN CARE FOR OTHERS.

BELIEVE THAT YOU'LL KNOW WHAT
SCHEDULE IS BEST FOR YOUR FAMILY.

YOU HAVE THE POWER TO CREATE
THE HOME YOU WANT FOR YOUR CHILDREN.

KEEP THE END IN MIND.

WE'RE BETTER TOGETHER.

YOU'VE GOT THIS, MAMA!

xx
Andrea